MW00439228

# THE
# AGONY OF JESUS

## IN THE GARDEN OF GETHSEMANE

*By*

St. Padre Pio
of Pietrelcina, O.F.M. CAP.

TAN Books
An Imprint of Saint Benedict Press, LLC
Charlotte, North Carolina

Imprimatur: ✠ JOANNES GREGORIUS MURRAY,
Archbishop Sancti Pauli
Paulopoli die 30a Novembris 1952

ISBN: 978-0-89555-097-2

Originally published by Fathers Rumble and Carty, Radio Replies Press, Inc., St. Paul, Minn. U.S.A.

*Complete and Unabridged*

Padre Pio celebrated the 50th anniversary of his stigmata on September 20, 1968. Three days later, on September 23, 1968, he passed away. Padre Pio was canonized on June 16, 2002.

The photographs used in this booklet are inserted with the permission of the copyright owner, Federico Abresch of San Giovanni Rotondo, Foggia, Italy.

Front cover photo courtesy of National Center for Padre Pio.

Printed in India

TAN Books
An Imprint of Saint Benedict Press, LLC
Charlotte, North Carolina
2013

# Editor's Foreword

Among some writings in my possession are those of a devout religious, to whom I am bound by the bond of blood, the priesthood and the Seraphic vocation as well as a common birthplace. They include this meditation on THE AGONY OF JESUS IN THE GARDEN OF GETHSEMANE, from which my spirit draws motives for an ever greater devotion to the most sacred Humanity of Christ. Certain that the spread of this meditation would produce much good in souls, who from the Passion of Jesus draw the daily food for their life of union with God, I believed that I would perform a meritorious deed in having it printed.

May Jesus suffering in the Garden find our hearts always ready to respond to the inspirations of grace in order to act in such a manner that all fulfill in their members as St. Paul says: ". . . what is lacking of the sufferings of Christ." (*Colossians* 1:24)

Fr. Ezechia Cardone, O.F.M.
Benevento, at St. Paschal, March 25, 1952.

# Translator's Preface

As mentioned in the Foreword of the Editor, the original manuscript of this meditation is in his possession. Fr. Ezechia is a cousin of Fr. Pio of Pietrelcina, O.F.M. Cap., the author, who wrote the meditation many years ago. Fr. Ezechia, wishing to share this treasure with others obtained the permission both of his superiors and of Fr. Pio to have it printed. He likewise gave the permission for the English translation and its publication.

When beginners in the spiritual life are first introduced to mental prayer they are taught methods, plans, etc. of meditation. First the preparatory prayer, then a vivid representation of a Gospel scene, which should be contemplated, considering persons, actions, words, possible emotions of those in the scene. From this consideration the soul proceeds to acts of love, contrition, humility, petition, resignation to God's Will, etc., as the subject matter may suggest. At the end comes the application and prayer for grace to practice some virtue.

Some, not understanding the nature of true prayer (which is conversation with God) make the big mistake of thinking that each of these parts must be kept as in an airtight compartment, one may not interfere with the other, none may overlap. Contemplating a scene, thinking over a truth is not yet prayer. In most cases it is a necessary preparation. It is fuel but it is not yet fire. When affections

3

arise the intellectual work should cease—even if this happens at the very beginning. When the affections seem to fade away, the mind turns again to the scene or truth—more fuel is sought for the fire— love. The consideration has its proper value. The deeper the impression, the deeper the affections, with the help of grace, of course. Thus the various so-called parts of the plan of meditation must be interwoven as the soul is moved by grace. After all prayer is a response to a movement of grace. It is a: "Yes, Father!" to an inspiration from above.

This meditation by Fr. Pio of Pietrelcina, O.F.M.Cap., is an excellent example of how the soul freely gives itself up to the movements of grace. Freely the various parts of meditation are interwoven; thoughts, affections, petitions flow naturally.

The beautiful preparatory prayer humbly beseeches the Holy Spirit for enlightenment and for an inflaming of the heart, to make a good meditation on the Passion of Christ. Our Sorrowful Mother is asked to guide him, and the Guardian Angel to guard his faculties in this prayer.

Each of the four parts begins with a picture of the scene. But that is not enough. Throughout the meditation we get glimpses of the unfolding of the drama, the most sacred and terrifying drama. The pictures live. Likewise the personal applications, acts of love, humility, contrition, submission to the Will of God come up again and again. A final prayer, resume of the divine tragedy, a petition to obtain the corresponding graces, closes the meditation.

Spiritual writers recommend that one try to identify oneself with the scene upon which one meditates, as if one were an actual witness. The author seems to see Christ, shudders at the inhumanity of the sufferings, suffers with the suffering Christ, speaks with Him, prays with Him.

But do not make this meditation a mere study on prayer. Read it prayerfully, live the scenes with the author, share in his devout aspirations, affections, petitions, and especially his acts of love for the Saviour. It is a signal grace to enter ever more deeply into the mysteries of the Passion of Christ.

The translation has been made as faithful as possible, considering, of course, both English and Italian idiom. But it falls far short of the beauty of the original.

The Translator

# THE AGONY OF JESUS

in the Garden of Gethsemane

*By*

Padre Pio of Pietrelcina, O.F.M. Cap.

Most Divine Spirit, enlighten and inflame me in meditating on the Passion of Jesus, help me to penetrate this mystery of love and suffering of a God, Who, clothed with our humanity, suffers, agonizes and dies for the love of the creature! ... The Eternal, the Immortal Who debases Himself to undergo an immense martyrdom, the ignominious death of the Cross, amidst insults, contempt and abuse, to save the creature which offended Him, and which wallows in the slime of sin. Man rejoices in his sin and his God is sad because of sin, suffers, sweats blood, amidst terrible agony of spirit. No, I cannot enter this wide ocean of love and pain unless Thou with Thy grace sustain me. Oh that I could penetrate to the innermost recesses of the Heart of Jesus to read there the essence of His bitterness, which brought Him to the point of death in the Garden; that I could comfort Him in the abandonment by His Father and His own. Oh that I could unite myself with Him in order to expiate with Him.

Mary, Mother of Sorrows, may I unite myself with Thee to follow Jesus and share His pains and Thy sufferings.

My Guardian Angel, guard my faculties and keep

6

**Stigmata of Padre Pio in 1918**

them recollected on Jesus suffering, so that they will not stray far from Him.

*   *   *

# I

Arriving at the close of His earthly life, the Divine Redeemer, after having given Himself entirely to us as food and drink in the Sacrament of His love, and having nourished His Apostles with His Body and Blood Soul and Divinity, went with His own to the Garden of Olives, known to His disciples and also to Judas. Along the road which leads from the Cenacle to the Garden, Jesus teaches His disciples. He prepares them for the impending separation, for His imminent Passion, and prepares them to undergo, for love of Him, calumnies, persecution and death itself, to fashion in themselves Him, Who is their model.

"I shall be with you" and do not be troubled, O disciples, because the Divine promise will not fail. You will have a proof of this in the present solemn hour.

He is there to begin His dolorous Passion. Instead of thinking of Himself, He is all anxiety for you.

Oh what an immensity of love does this Heart contain! His face is covered with sadness and at the same time with love. His words proceed from His innermost Heart. He speaks with a profusion of affection, encouragement, comfort, and in comforting gives His promise. He explains the most profound mysteries of His Passion.

This journey of Thine, O Jesus, has always touched my heart with an increase of love so profound and so deep for those who love Thee, with increase of love that hurries to immolate itself for others, to ransom them from slavery. Thou hast

**Padre Pio in 1935**

taught that there is no greater proof of love than to lay down one's life for one's friends. And now Thou art about to put this seal on the proof of Thine own life. Who would not be overawed by such an oblation?

Arriving at the Garden the Divine Master withdrew apart from His disciples, taking along only three of them, Peter, James and John, to have them as witnesses of His sufferings. Would just these three, who had seen Him transfigured on Tabor between Moses and Elias, and who had confessed Him to be God, would they now have the strength to acknowledge the Man-God in pain and mortal anguish?

Entering the Garden He told them: "Remain here. Watch and pray that you enter not into temptation!" Be on your guard, He seems to say to them, because the enemy is not asleep. Arm yourself against him beforehand, with the weapon of prayer, so that you may not become involved and led into sin. It is the hour of darkness. Having thus admonished them he separates Himself from them about a stone's throw and prostrates Himself on the ground.

He is extremely sad; His soul is a prey of indescribable bitterness. The night is advanced and bright. The moon shines in the sky, leaving shadows in the Garden. It seems to throw a sinister brightness, a foreboding of the grave and dreadful events to come, which make the blood tremble and freeze in the veins—it seems as if stained with blood. A wind, like the forerunner of the coming tempest agitates the olive trees and, together with the rustling of the leaves penetrates to the bones, like a messenger of death, descending into the soul and filling it with deadly grief.

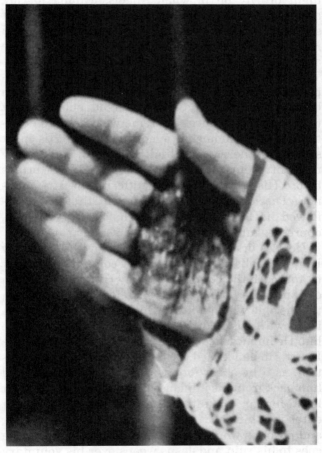

**Stigmatized Right Hand**

Night most horrible, like which there will never be another!

What a contrast, O Jesus! How beautiful was the night of Thy birth, when Angels, leaping for joy, announced peace, singing the Gloria. And now, it seems to me, they surround Thee sadly, keeping at a respectful distance, as if respecting the supreme anguish of Thy spirit.

This is the place where Jesus came to pray. He deprived his most sacred humanity of the strength bestowed on it by His Divine Person, submitting it to indefinable sadness, extreme weakness, to dejection and abandonment, to mortal anguish. His spirit swims in these as a limitless ocean, and every moment seems about to be submerged. It brings before His spirit the entire sufferings of His imminent Passion, which, like a torrent that has overflowed its banks, pours into His Heart, torments, oppresses and submerges it in a sea of grief.

He sees first Judas, His disciple, loved so much by Him who sells Him for just a few coins; who is about to approach the Garden to betray Him and give Him over into the hands of His enemies. He! The friend, the disciple whom a little while before He had nourished with His Body and Blood . . . prostrate before him He had washed his feet and pressed them to His Heart. He had kissed those feet with brotherly affection, as if by sheer force of love He wanted to hold him back from his impious, sacrilegious design, or at least, having committed the insane deed, he might enter into himself, recalling so many proofs of love, and perhaps would repent and be saved. But no, he goes to his ruin and Jesus weeps over his voluntary perdition.

He sees Himself bound and dragged by His ene-

**Meditation before Mass**

mies through the streets of Jerusalem, through those very streets through which only a few days before He passed triumphantly acclaimed as the Messiah . . . He sees Himself before the High Priest beaten, declared guilty of death. He, the author of life also sees Himself led from one tribunal to another, into the presence of judges who condemn Him.

He sees His own people, so loved by Him, the recipients of so many of His benefits, who now maltreat Him with infernal howls and hissing, and with a great shout demand His death—the death on the Cross. He hears their unjust accusations, sees Himself condemned to the most awful scourging; crowned with thorns, derided, saluted as a mock-king and struck.

Finally He sees Himself condemned to the ignominious death of the Cross, then ascending to Calvary, fainting under the weight of the cross, pale and falling to the ground repeatedly. He sees Himself, arrived on Calvary, despoiled of His garments, stretched out on the Cross, pitilessly crucified, raised up on it in the sight of all. He hangs on the nails which cause excruciating torture . . . Oh God, what a long agony of three hours will overwhelm Him amidst the insults of a crazed, heartless crowd.

He sees His throat and entrails on fire with a burning thirst, and to add to this agony, a drink of vinegar and gall. He sees the abandonment of His Father and the desolation of His Mother.

At the end, the ignominious death between two robbers; the one to acknowledge and confess Him as God and be saved, the other to blaspheme and insult Him and die in despair.

He sees Longinus approach and, as a final insult

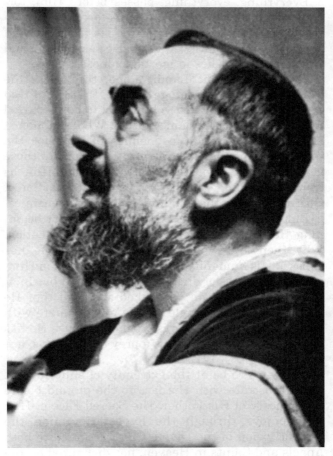

**Offertory**

and contempt, pierce His side. Christ beholds the consummation of humiliation in the separation of soul and body.

Everything, everything, passes before Him, torments Him, terrifies Him, and this terror takes possession of Him, overwhelms Him. He trembles as if shaken by a violent fever. Fear also seizes Him, and His spirit languishes in mortal sadness.

He, the innocent Lamb, alone, thrown to the wolves, without any refuge . . . He, the Son of God . . . the Lamb dedicated voluntarily to be sacrificed for the glory of the same Father Who abandoned Him to the fury of the enemies of God, for the redemption of the human race; forsaken by those very disciples who shamefully flee from Him as from a most dangerous being. He, the Eternal Son of God has become the laughing-stock of His enemies.

But, will He retreat? . . . No, from the very beginning He embraces everything without reservation. Why then and whence this terror? Ah! He has exposed His humanity as a target to take upon Himself all the blows of divine justice offended by sin.

Vividly He feels in His naked spirit all that He must suffer; every single sin He must expiate with each single pain, and He is crushed because He has given over His humanity as a prey to weakness, terror, fear.

He seems to be at the extremity of suffering . . . He is prostrate with His face to the ground before the majesty of His Father. The Sacred Face of Him Who enjoys through the hypostatic union the beatific vision of the Divine Glory accorded to both Angels and Saints in Heaven, lies disfigured on the ground. My God! My Jesus! Art Thou not the God of Heaven and earth, equal in all things to Thy Father,

16

**Offering the Chalice**

Who humiliates Thee to the point of losing even the semblance of man?

Ah Yes! I understand. It is to teach me, proud man, that to deal with Heaven I must abase myself down to the center of the earth. It is to repair and expiate for my haughtiness, that Thou bowest down thus before Thy Father. It is to direct His pitying glance upon humanity, which has turned away from Him by rebellion. It is because of Thy humiliation that He forgives the proud creature. It is in order to reconcile earth with Heaven, that Thou abasest Thyself down to it, as if to give it the kiss of peace. O Jesus, mayest Thou be blessed and thanked always and by all men for all Thy mortifications and humiliations by which Thou hast atoned for us to God to Whom Thou has united us in the embrace of holy love!

\* \* \*

## II

Jesus rises and turns His sad and suppliant glance to Heaven. He raises His arms and prays. My God, with what deadly pallor that face is suffused! He prays to that Father Who seems to have turned away His glance and Who appears ready to strike Him with His sword of vengeance. He prays with all the confidence of a Son, but He fully understands the position He holds. He realizes that it is He alone, as a victim for the human race, Who bears the odium of having outraged the Divine Majesty. He realizes that He alone through the sacrifice of His life can satisfy divine justice and reconcile the creature with the Creator. He wants it, and wants it efficaciously. But nature is crushed at the sight of His bitter Passion. Nature revolts against the sacrifice.

on the altar. Partly in shadow, this image cap-
tures a moment of intense contemplation, his
attention fixed on what he reads before him in
prayer.

**Holding Paten**

But His spirit is ready for the immolation, and He continues the battle with all His strength. He feels Himself cast down but He perseveres in the oblation of Himself.

My Jesus, how can we obtain strength from Thee, if we see Thee so weak and crushed?

Yes, I understand. Thou hast taken all our weakness upon Thyself. And to give us Thy strength Thou hast become the scape-goat. It is to teach us that we must place our trust only in Thee in the struggles of life, even when it seems as if Heaven were closed to us.

Jesus, in agony cries to His Father: "If it is possible, take this chalice from Me!" It is the cry of nature which, weighted down, confidently has recourse to Heaven for assistance. Although He knows that He will not be heard, because He wants it thus, He prays. My Jesus, why dost Thou ask that which Thou knowest will not be granted? SUFFERING AND LOVE.

Behold the great secret. The pain which oppresses Thee urges Thee to seek help and comfort, but the love to satisfy divine justice and give us back to God makes Thee cry out: "Not Mine, but Thy Will be done!" To this prayer Divine Justice exacts the sacrifice necessary to repair the injury to God.

His desolate Heart has need of comfort. The desolation in which He finds Himself, the battle which He is fighting alone, seems to make Him go in search of someone who could comfort Him. Slowly, therefore, He rises from the ground and, staggering takes a few steps. He approaches His disciples in search of comfort. They, having lived so long with Him, they, His confidants, could well understand His internal grief. And with this expectation He goes to

**Blessing the Host**

21

them. They will surely know how to provide a little comfort for Him.

But oh, what a disillusionment! He finds them buried in profound sleep and feels Himself so much more alone in that limitless solitude of His Spirit. He approaches them and, sweetly turning to Peter, He says: "Simon, dost Thou sleep? Thou who didst protest that thou didst want to follow Me unto death?" And turning to the others He adds: "Could you not watch one hour with me?" The lament of the Lamb destined for sacrifice; of a wounded Heart that suffers immensely . . . alone, without comfort. He, however, raises Himself as if from a battlefield, and forgetting Himself and His sufferings, concerned only for them, adds: "Watch and pray that you fall not into temptation." He seems to say: If you have so quickly forgotten Me, Who struggle and suffer, at least watch and pray for yourselves.

They, however, heavy with sleep, hardly hear the voice of Jesus, they barely perceive Him as a faint shadow, so much so that they are not aware of His countenance all disfigured from the internal agony which tortures Him.

O Jesus, how many generous souls wounded by this complaint have kept Thee company in the Garden, sharing Thy bitterness and Thy mortal anguish . . . How many hearts in the course of the centuries have responded generously to Thy invitation . . . May this multitude of souls, then, in this supreme hour be a comfort to Thee, who, better than the disciples, share with Thee the distress of Thy heart, and cooperate with Thee for their own salvation and that of others. And grant that I also may be of their number, that I also may offer Thee some relief.

**Adoring**

23

### III

Jesus has returned to His place of prayer and another picture, more terrible than the first presents itself to Him. All our sins with their entire ugliness parade before Him in every detail. He sees all the meanness and the malice of creatures in committing them. He knows to what extent these sins offend and outrage the Majesty of God. He sees all the infamies, immodesties, blasphemies which proceed from the lips of creatures accompanied by the malice of their hearts, of those hearts and those lips which were created to bring forth hymns of praise and benediction to the Creator. He sees the sacrileges with which priests and faithful defile themselves, not caring about those Sacraments instituted for our salvation as necessary means for it; now, instead, made an occasion of sin and damnation of souls. He must clothe Himself with this entire unclean mass of human corruption and present Himself before the sanctity of His Father, to expiate everything with individual pains, to render Him all that glory of which they have robbed Him; to cleanse that human cesspool in which man wallows with contemptible indifference.

And all this does not make Him retreat. As a raging sea this mass inundates Him, enfolds Him, oppresses Him. Behold Him before His Father the God of Justice, facing the full penalty of divine justice. He, the essence of purity, sanctity by nature, in contact with sin! . . . Indeed, as if He Himself had become a sinner. Who can fathom the disgust that He feels in His innermost spirit? The horror He feels? The nausea, the contempt He senses so

**Memento of the Dead**

vividly? And having taken all upon Himself, nothing excepted, He is crushed by this immense weight, oppressed, thrown down, prostrated. Exhausted he groans beneath the weight of divine justice, before His Father, Who has permitted His Son to offer Himself as a Victim for sin, as one accursed.

He would fain shake off this immense burden that crushes Him—He would fain free Himself of this horrible load which makes Him shudder—His own purity rejects it—the very glance of the avenging Father, Who abandons Him in these muddy, putrid waters of guilt with which He sees Himself covered—All this rushes to His Spirit urging Him to draw back from the bitter Passion. The revulsion of His Divinity against sin adds to the conflict within His human soul. All instinct counsels that He unburden Himself of these infamies, rejecting the very thought of them. But the consideration of unvindicated justice and the unreconciled sinner predominates in His heart full of love. These two forces, these two loves, one more holy than the other, struggle for victory in the Heart of the Saviour. Which will conquer? Without doubt He wants to give victory to offended justice. This gains over all else and He wants this to triumph. But what a spectacle must He represent? That of a man soiled with the filth of humanity. He, essential sanctity, to see himself filthy with sin, even if only in outward appearance? This, No! This terrifies Him, makes Him tremble, crushes Him.

To find support in this terrible conflict He gives Himself over to prayer. Prostrate before the majesty of His Father, He says: "Father, take this chalice from Me!" It is as if He said: My Father, I want Thy glory, I want Thy justice to be fully satisfied. I want

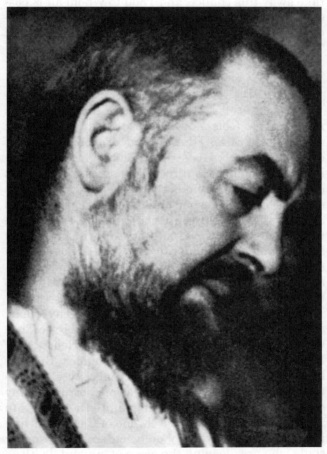

**Pouring Wine into Chalice**

the human family to be reconciled with Thee. But that I, Who am sanctity itself, should see Myself defiled by sin, Ah! Not this! Take away, therefore, take away this chalice, and Thou to Whom all is possible, find in the infinite treasures of Thy Holy Wisdom another means. But if Thou dost not want this: "Not my Will but Thine be done!"

\* \* \*

## IV

And again this time the prayer of the Saviour has no effect. He feels as if He were about to die. With difficulty He raises Himself from prayer in search of comfort. He feels His strength ebbing away. Tottering and grasping He directs His steps towards His disciples. Again He finds them sleeping. At this His sadness becomes deeper, and He is content merely to awaken them. What confusion must have overcome them! But Jesus says nothing this time. He only seems immensely sadder to me . . . He keeps to Himself all the bitterness and pain of this abandonment and indifference. By His silence He seems to sympathize with the weakness of His own.

O Jesus, how much pain I read in Thy Heart already full to overflowing with distress. I see Thee withdraw from Thy disciples cut to the Heart. Ah if I could give Thee some relief, some comfort. But, not knowing what else to do I weep at Thy side. The tears of my love for Thee and of my sorrow for my sins, conscious of Thy suffering, unite themselves to Thine. They can rise to the throne of the Father and incline Him to have pity on Thee and on so many souls who are sleeping the sleep of sin and death.

Again Jesus returns to His place of prayer, afflicted, weakened. He falls rather than prostrates

**Ecce Agnus Dei**

Himself. A mortal anguish overwhelms Him and He prays more intensely. The Father turns away His glance as if He were the most abject of men.

I seem to hear all the laments of the Saviour: Oh if at least man, for whom I am in anguish and for whom I am ready to embrace all, could only be *grateful,* would respond to the graces I obtain for him by My great suffering for him! If he would only esteem the value of the price I pay to ransom him from the death of sin, to bestow on him the true life of the sons of God. Ah, that love which grieves My Heart more cruelly than the executioners will tear my flesh! . . . Oh no! He sees man who does not know because he does not want to draw profit from it. He will even blaspheme this Divine Blood, and more irreparable and inexcusable still, will turn It to his damnation. Only a few will profit by It, the greater number run the way of perdition.

And in the great distress of His Heart He continues to repeat: "Quae utilitas in sanguine meo! What profit is there in My Blood!" But even the thought of these few urges His Heart to continue to endure the conflict, to face all the sufferings of His Passion and Death to obtain for them the palm of victory.

There remains nothing to which He can turn to find comfort—Heaven is closed to Him! Man, although he lies dying under the mass of sin, is ungrateful, ignores His love for him! He writhes in profound agony, love submerges Him, tortures Him—His countenance has deathly pallor—His eyes are languid, an undefinable sadness takes entire possession of Him! "My soul is sorrowful unto death."

Divine Blood, spontaneously Thou flowest from the loving Heart of my Jesus; the flood of pain, the

**Last Blessing**

31

extreme bitterness, the steadfast perseverance which He sustains press Thee from that Heart, and sweating from His pores Thou dost flow to wash the earth! . . . Let me gather Thee up, Divine Blood, especially these first drops. I want to keep Thee in the chalice of my heart. It is the most convincing proof that love alone has drawn Thee from the veins of my Jesus! I want to purify myself with Thee, and all the places contaminated by sin. I want to offer Thee to the Father.

It is the Blood of His well beloved Son, Who came down to purify the earth; It is the Blood of His Son, the God-Man, which ascends to His throne to pacify His justice, offended by our sins. He is superabundantly satisfied.

What am I saying? If the justice of the Father has been satisfied, is Jesus not sated with suffering? No, Jesus does not want to stop the flow of His charity for them. Men must have the infinite proof of His love. He must see to what ignominy it can make Him go. If the infinite justice of the Father is measured by the infinite value of His Most Precious Blood and He is satisfied, man, on his part must have palpable proof that His love is not yet sated with suffering, and that He will not stop, but continue to the extreme agony of the Cross, to the ignominious death on it.

Perhaps a spiritually minded man can evaluate at least in part, the love which reduces Him to the agony of the Garden. But he who lives, given up to material affairs, seeking more the world than Heaven must see Him also agonizing and dying outwardly on the Cross, to be moved by the sight of His Blood and of this torturing agony.

No, His loving Heart is not satisfied. Regaining

**Last Blessing**

consciousness, He prays again: "Father if Thou dost not wish that this chalice pass from Me, unless I drink it, not Mine but Thy Will be done."

From now on Jesus responds to the loving cry of His Heart, to the cry of humanity, which, in order to be redeemed clamors for His death. At the sentence of death which His Father pronounces against Him heaven and earth demand His death. Jesus, resigned, bends His adorable head: "Father, if Thou dost not want that this chalice pass unless I drink it, not Mine but Thy Will be done."

Behold He sends an Angel, an Angel-Messenger, to comfort Jesus. What motives of comfort, of relief does the Angel offer to the strong God, Lord of the Universe, the Invincible, the Omnipotent! . . . But He has become subject to suffering, He has taken upon Himself our weakness; it is the man who suffers, and is in agony. It is the miracle of His infinite love which makes him sweat Blood and brings upon Him this agony.

The prayer to His Father has two motives, one for Himself, the other for us. His Father does not hear Him for His own sake, but wants Him to die for us. I believe that the Angel bows reverently before Jesus, before this Eternal beauty, now covered with blood and dust, and with deferential honor imparts that consolation of resignation of the human will to the Divine Will, beseeching Him for the glory of the Father and in the name of all sinners to drink that chalice which was offered to Him from Eternity for their salvation. He has prayed to teach us also that when our soul finds itself in desolation like His, we should seek consolation from Heaven only in prayer to sustain us in the sacrifice.

He, our strength will be ready to assist us because

**Padre Pio as Deacon**

He had willed to take upon Himself our miseries.

Yes, O Jesus, it is for Thee to drink the chalice to the dregs, Thou art now vowed to the most terrible death. Jesus, may nothing be able to separate me from Thee, neither life nor death. Following Thee in life, affectionately bound to Thy suffering may it be granted to me to expire with Thee on Calvary in order to ascend, with Thee to glory; to follow Thee in tribulations and persecutions, to be made worthy one day to come to love Thee in the unveiled glory of Heaven; to sing to Thee the hymn of thanksgiving for Thy great suffering.

But look! Jesus raises Himself from the ground, strong, invincible as a lion in battle; behold now that Jesus, Who longingly had desired this banquet of blood, "with desire have I desired," He shakes the disarray from His noble head, wipes the Bloody Sweat from His face, and resolutely goes towards the entrance of the Garden.

Where art Thou going, Jesus? Art Thou not that Jesus I saw languishing in Thy soul, a prey to terror, fatigue, fear, discouragement, desolation? Whom I saw trembling, crushed under the immense weight of the evils which were about to overcome Thee? Where art Thou going now so ready, so resolute, so full of courage? To whom art Thou exposing Thyself?

Oh! I hear it! The weapon of prayer has helped Me conquer, and the spirit has subjected the weakness of nature to itself. In prayer have I obtained strength and now I can face everything. Follow My example and deal with Heaven with the same confidence as I have done.

Jesus approaches the three Apostles. They are still sleeping. Strong emotion, the late hour of the

**Palm Sunday**

night, that presentiment of something awful—irreparable —which seemed to be approaching, and fatigue, had put them to sleep, such a sleep that weighs down upon one and seems impossible to shake off, and trying to shake it off, one falls into it again without knowing how. Jesus has pity on them saying: "The spirit is willing but the flesh is weak."

Jesus has so felt this neglect from His own that He exclaims: "Sleep now and rest." He pauses a moment. Suddenly, at the footsteps of Jesus, with an effort they open their eyes. Then Jesus continues: "It is enough. The hour is at hand. The Son of Man will be betrayed into the hands of sinners. Rise, let us go. Behold, he who betrays Me is at hand." (*Matthew* 26:45, 46).

Jesus beholds everything with His all-seeing glance. He seems to say: You who are My friends and disciples sleep, but My enemies are awake and are about to seize Me. You, Peter, who felt strong enough to follow Me unto death, you sleep! From the beginning you gave Me proofs of weakness. But be calm, I clothed Myself with weakness and I have prayed for you. And after you have recognized your mistake, I will be your strength and you will feed My lambs . . . You, John, also sleep! You, who a few hours past in the ecstasy of My love, have felt the beat of this Heart, you also sleep? Rise, let us go, there is no more time to sleep, the enemy is at the gate; it is the hour of the power of darkness, yes, let us go. I go spontaneously to meet death. Judas hurries to betray Me and I advance with firm and sure step. I will place no obstacle to the fulfillment of the prophecies. My hour has come; the hour of great mercy for humanity.

And, in fact, there is heard the sound of steps, a

**Recent Picture of Padre Pio in
Monastery Gardens**

reddish light of torches penetrates the Garden and Jesus, followed by the three disciples, advances, intrepid and calm.

### (Concluding Prayer)

O Jesus, impart to me also that same strength, when my weak nature foreseeing future evils rebels, so that like Thou, I may accept with serene peace and tranquility all the pains and distress which I may meet on this earth of exile. I unite all to Thy merits, to Thy pains, Thy expiations, Thy tears, that I may cooperate with Thee for my salvation and flee from sin, which was the sole cause of making Thee sweat blood and which led Thee to death. Destroy in me everything that does not please Thee, and with the sacred fire of Thy love write Thy sufferings into my heart. Hold me so closely to Thee, with a bond so tight and so sweet, that I shall never again abandon Thee in Thy sufferings.

May I be able to rest on Thy Heart to obtain comfort in the sufferings of life. May my spirit have no other desire but to live at Thy side in the Garden and unite itself to the pains of Thy Heart. May my soul be inebriated with Thy Blood and feed itself with the bread of Thy sufferings. Amen.

# NOTES

# NOTES

# NOTES

# NOTES